MONSTER MANIA

WITCHES

John Malam

QEB Publishing

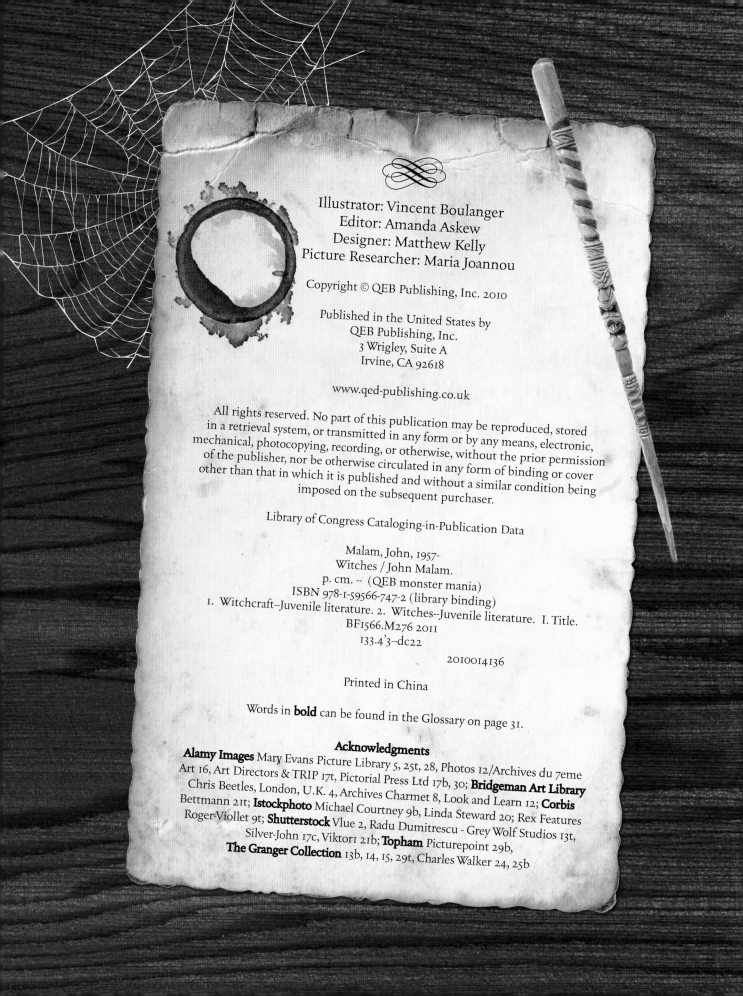

Illustrator: Vincent Boulanger
Editor: Amanda Askew
Designer: Matthew Kelly
Picture Researcher: Maria Joannou

Published in the United States by
QEB Publishing, Inc.
3 Wrigley, Suite A
Irvine, CA 92618

www.qed-publishing.co.uk

Library of Congress Cataloging-in-Publication Data

Malam, John, 1957-
Witches / John Malam.
p. cm. -- (QEB monster mania)
ISBN 978-1-59566-747-2 (library binding)
1. Witchcraft--Juvenile literature. 2. Witches--Juvenile literature. I. Title.
BF1566.M276 2011
133.4'3--dc22

2010014136

Printed in China

Words in **bold** can be found in the Glossary on page 31.

Acknowledgments

Alamy Images Mary Evans Picture Library 5, 25t, 28, Photos 12/Archives du 7eme
Art 16, Art Directors & TRIP 17t, Pictorial Press Ltd 17b, 30; **Bridgeman Art Library**
Chris Beetles, London, U.K. 4, Archives Charmet 8, Look and Learn 12; **Corbis**
Bettmann 21t; **Istockphoto** Michael Courtney 9b, Linda Steward 20; Rex Features
Roger-Viollet 9t; **Shutterstock** Vlue 2, Radu Dumitrescu - Grey Wolf Studios 13t,
Silver-John 17c, Viktor1 21b; **Topham** Picturepoint 29b,
The Granger Collection 13b, 14, 15, 29t, Charles Walker 24, 25b

CONTENTS

A WORLD OF WITCHES

Who or what are witches? Old stories are full of these troublesome creatures. They cast spells and curses, change their shape, make themselves invisible, fly through the sky, and cause wild storms. They have the power to harm, and the power to heal.

At **Halloween** many people pretend to be witches, dressing up in capes and pointed hats, going from house to house to play trick or treat. It was not like this in the past. In those days, people were scared of witches. They were thought to be evil and were hunted. Thousands were accused of being witches, and were put to death.

Halloween

Also known as All Hallows Eve, the night of October 31 is when witches, fairies, ghosts, and other spirits are free to roam the human world. It comes from the ancient festival of **Samhain**, which was held long ago to mark the start of winter.

With her pointed hat, wand, bubbling **cauldron** and black cats, she has to be a witch.

WHO'S WHO AMONG WITCHES?

GOOD AND BAD WITCHES

Stories describe different kinds of witch. The most common type is said to be a woman with evil, harmful powers. She could be any age, but if she is very old and ugly, she is a **hag** witch. But not all witches were bad. For example, a witch known as a **wise woman** or a white witch knew about herbs and potions, and used them for healing.

AND THE REST...

MYTHOLOGICAL WITCHES

Witches in myths, such as Hecate and her daughter Circe, whom the ancient Greeks told stories about.

FICTIONAL WITCHES

Made-up witches, such as the famous three witches in Shakespeare's play *Macbeth*.

CUNNING MAN

Like a wise woman, the cunning man was said to be a healer, who used his magic only for the good of others.

THE WITCH WHO
Turned Men into Pigs

The ancient Greek enchantress Circe was young, beautiful, and used magic. These were the things men knew about her, and these were the things that Circe used against men.

It happened that a ship carrying the hero Odysseus was passing by Circe's island, heading home to Greece. Tired and hungry after a long voyage, his men went ashore.

They followed the sound of Circe's gentle singing, and when they came to her house she gave them food. However, Circe had mixed a potion into the food, and the men were turned into pigs.

As they ate the charmed food, Circe's potion did its evil work.

Odysseus, who had stayed safely behind on his ship, set out to fight Circe. On the way, the god Hermes gave him a potion to break Circe's spells. With sword in hand, Odysseus threatened to strike her dead. In return for sparing her, Circe promised to change the pigs back into men. Odysseus had defeated the power of evil, and was now free to carry on with his journey.

Goddess of witches

The ancient Greeks believed that the most evil witch was Hecate, the goddess of magic. She roamed the night with a pack of red-eyed hell hounds. She was so scary, that people refused to call her by her name. Instead, they called her "The Nameless One".

Odysseus, who was safe from Circe's magic, forced the witch to bring his men back.

Howling dogs

Hecate was said to be invisible to the human eye. Only dogs could see this witch, and when you hear dogs howling, it's because they have seen her.

This story comes from
ANCIENT GREECE

The powers of
WITCHES

Witches are creatures with great powers. Some were feared because their powers were thought to be linked to the forces of evil. However, others were respected for their wisdom because they put their powers to good use.

STORMY WEATHER

Storms, bad weather, and crop damage were said to be the work of witches. The power to destroy crops was called **blasting**. A witch would burn the body of a toad or a snake until it turned to ash. If the ash was scattered across a field, nothing would grow there.

CASTING SPELLS

Witches are best known for their power of magic to make both good and bad things happen. Perhaps their most obvious use of magic is in casting spells —secret words that can be spoken or written down.

As she mixes a potion, a witch chants, "Double, double toil and trouble; fire burn, and cauldron bubble."

With her black cats to keep her company, a witch takes to the skies on her broomstick.

THE POWER TO FLY

Witches are said to mix magical potions, such as flying ointment. Bat's blood and poisonous plants were mixed together in a cauldron until they became sorcerer's grease. They smeared it on their skin, or on broomsticks, shovels, forks, or the backs of animals. Whatever it touched, then had the power of flight.

Flying broomsticks

In old folk tales, witches fly through the sky on broomsticks. It's hard to say how the idea started. Perhaps it is because if a woman was away from her house, she would leave her broomstick outside the door to say she was not at home. Superstitious people imagined she used the broom to fly on.

9

The Man Ridden by a WITCH

It was soon to be Walpurgis Night, the night when all the witches in Germany flew to the Brocken, a high mountain in the north. A man boasted that if a witch flew close to him, he would knock her from her broomstick. The old woman next door told him to be careful, as a witch might hear him. He took no notice.

Witches' night arrived, and the man went to work. Suddenly, a swarm of witches swooped down on him. One came close, and he tried to knock her to the ground, but the old hag was too quick for him. In an instant, she pushed him over and rode him into the sky, like a broomstick.

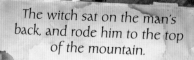

The witch sat on the man's back, and rode him to the top of the mountain.

He looked at her wrinkled, old face, and saw she was the witch.

The next day, when the man was back at home, the old woman came to him again. Although she had been his neighbor for many years, he had not taken much notice of her—until now.

"I told you a witch might hear you boasting!" she cackled. The man looked closely at the old woman, and realized that she was the witch who had ridden him! Her secret was out, and she was taken away to be punished.

This story comes from
GERMANY

Cats and other FAMILIARS

It was said that every witch had at least one **familiar** or imp. They were given to the witch by the devil, or bought from another witch. Familiars had the form of an animal. Cats, dogs, toads and owls were the most common types of familiar, but even something as small as a fly could be a witch's helper.

Witches treated their familiars with great care, as if they were much-loved pets. They made them welcome in their homes, fed them, and gave them names such as Greedigut. Every familiar was a cunning imp that delighted in carrying out the witch's instructions. Most of the time, familiars acted as spies, gathering information for the witch.

With her familiar looking on, a witch practices her magic.

In return for doing the witch's work, a familiar demanded milk or, better still, blood. The best blood of all was the witch's own. She would prick her finger to make it bleed, and her familiar would suck at her precious blood. Sometimes it might suck from a spot on her body, leaving a telltale witch mark for all to see.

A witch fed her familiar with drops of her own blood.

Unlucky black cats

Cats have been linked with witches for centuries. They are the most common form of familiar. When they vanish for hours at a time, it's because they've been sent out to spy. There was a time in Europe when black cats were hunted and killed because they were said to be the devil himself.

Elizabeth Clark's familiars

Elizabeth Clark was an Englishwoman accused of being a witch in the 1600s. She said she had five familiars living with her:
- *Holt, a kitten*
- *Jamara, a fat, legless spaniel*
- *Sack and Sugar, a black rabbit*
- *Newes, a polecat*
- *Vinegar Tom, a houndlike creature with long legs and the head of an ox*

13

THE SALEM WITCHES

In the small town of Salem, in 1692, a group of teenage girls listened to Tituba, a slave girl from the island of Barbados. She told them stories about the islanders' belief in the spirit world.

They started telling each other's fortunes and as the days passed, the girls started acting strangely. Salem was a deeply religious Christian community, and the belief in witches was very real. Soon, people suspected a witch had taken control of the girls, and a hunt began to find out who it was.

The Salem witch trials have become famous, because so many people were accused of being witches.

The girls could have told the truth about their games, but it was too late. Things had become serious, and everyone was gripped by the fear of a witch living among them. The girls started to name names. More than one hundred people were arrested, including Tituba. Trials were held, and fourteen women and six men were put to death for being witches.

As for the girls whose game had led to the biggest witch-hunt in American history, they had to live with their secret for the rest of their lives. And Tituba? Her life was spared. She left Salem, and was never heard of again.

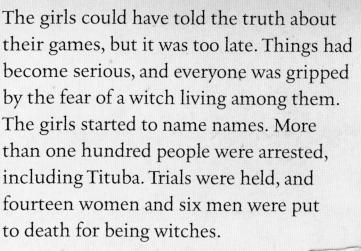

This story comes from
MASSACHUSETTS

The guilty were hanged by the neck until they were dead.

Ghosts of Salem

Of the twenty people executed as witches, nineteen of them were hanged on Gallows Hill. The twentieth victim was pressed to death by heavy rocks. According to legend, the ghosts of the victims haunt the area to this day.

THE TOOLS USED BY WITCHES

According to stories, witches used tools to do their work. Perhaps the most obvious tool for a witch was her familiar. This imp, which was often a cat, was a living tool that carried out the witch's instructions.

WOODEN WAND

No witch could be without her wand. It was a straight stick of hazel wood, about 17 inches (45 centimeters) long. The witch may have cut the stick herself, going out at full Moon to choose the best piece. Then she would shape it until it came to a long, tapering point. As she cast her spells, she moved her wand through the air. She held it with both hands as if gathering energy together to make her spells really powerful.

Witch's ladder

A **witch's ladder** was a short rope with knots tied in it. As the witch recited her spell or mixed her potion, she would tie and untie the knots. She spat on each knot to seal it. It was thought that each knot trapped the energy of a spell, and the only way to break the magic was by finding the ladder and untying the knots.

DOUBLE-EDGED KNIFE

A witch also used an **athame**. This was a double-edged knife. It was not used for cutting. Instead, the witch used it to direct her magical power, in the same way she used her wand.

SPELL BOOK AND CAULDRON

Before she cast a spell, a witch burned incense. Its scent filled the room and cleaned the air. She might also ring a bell, whose chiming sound was thought to drive harmful forces away. After this she would open her **grimoire** (say: grim-wor), which was her book of spells and magic. She would recite their words, tie knots in her witch's ladder, and mix ingredients together in her cauldron.

The Wizard of Oz (1939) features two witches: the Wicked Witch of the West, shown here with Dorothy and the Good Witch of the North.

17

An army turned to STONE

Long ago a great army came to England whose leader wanted to rule the country. As he fought his way across the land, he came to a place called Rollright, where a cunning witch lived. When the warrior asked her if he would ever conquer England, she set him a challenge.

The witch told him to take seven strides to the top of a nearby hill. Then, if he could see the village of Long Compton, he would indeed become England's king. It seemed an easy task, and as he strode away he called out:

"Stick, stock, stone,

As King of England I shall be known."

The warrior thought the witch's challenge would be easy to do—but she had tricked him.

But, the witch had tricked him. On the seventh stride, his view was blocked by another hill, and the village was nowhere to be seen. The witch cackled and said,

"As Long Compton thou canst not see
King of England thou shalt not be.
Rise up stick, and stand still stone,
For King of England thou shalt be none;
Thou and thy men hoar stones shall be
And I myself an eldern tree."

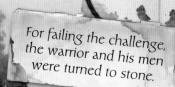

For failing the challenge, the warrior and his men were turned to stone.

The warrior was turned to stone. To this day, that stone is known as the King Stone, and his men are the standing stones that form the circle known as the Rollright Stones, in the county of Oxfordshire, England.

Stones with holes

Little stones with holes through them are known as **hagstones** or witch-stones. Superstitious people would hang these holed stones around the house. They believed they would prevent a witch from entering the house.

How to spot a WITCH

One of the most obvious signs was a so-called **witch mark**. It showed up as a blemish, a wart, or a mole on a person's skin. It was said to be where a witch's familiar had sucked her blood, sucking so hard it had left a mark.

WITCH MARK

People with such marks went to great trouble to hide them in case they were accused of being witches. They covered them up and even cut them off, but this only made scars, which were also said to be witch marks.

If a person was accused of having a witch mark, the next step was to prick it with a needle or pin. It was thought that a witch mark would not bleed when pricked. If no blood appeared, they were a witch and sent for trial. However, if there was blood, the person was innocent and was released.

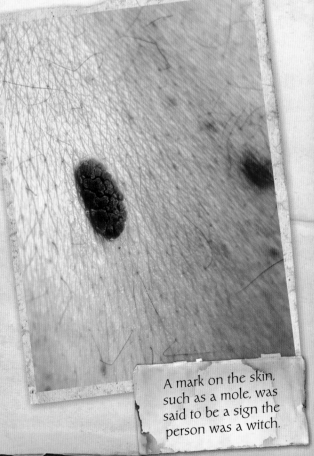

A mark on the skin, such as a mole, was said to be a sign the person was a witch.

People accused of being witches were ducked under water for a few minutes, before being brought back up, gasping for air.

SINK OR SWIM?

Swimming or **ducking** was another method used to detect a witch. The person was tied in a particular way, such as right thumb to left big toe. They were thrown into a river or a lake, and if they floated it was taken as a sign of guilt because the devil must have been helping them to survive. But, if they sank, they were innocent. Unfortunately, if the innocent person wasn't pulled out in time, they drowned.

Salt spotter

Salt was also used as a witch detector. It was thought that witches could not eat anything that had been salted, so accused people were given salty food to eat. If they choked or were sick, a witch had been found.

The Old Witch of the WOODS

Once upon a time, a boy and a girl lived with their loving father and wicked stepmother, who tried to get rid of them. One day she promised that they would find a kind woman in the forest to take care of them.

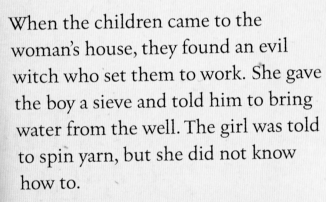
The boy thought he had been given an impossible task—he could not fill the sieve with water.

When the children came to the woman's house, they found an evil witch who set them to work. She gave the boy a sieve and told him to bring water from the well. The girl was told to spin yarn, but she did not know how to.

As the boy tried to fill the sieve, water poured through the holes. A flock of birds offered to help in exchange for bread and they told the boy to block the holes with clay. The girl was saved by mice, who in return for food, did the spinning for her. The witch was pleased.

That night, the children ran away, but the witch chased after them on her broomstick. When the witch was almost upon them, the girl turned and threw a comb at her. When the comb touched the ground, its teeth became trees that grew so tangled and crooked, the witch could not fly through them. The children escaped.

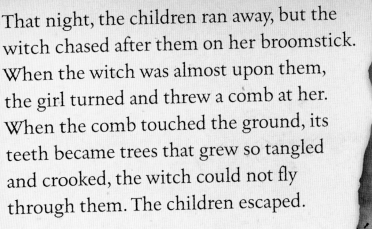

The witch's many hats

Pictures of witches often show them wearing tall, pointed black hats with wide brims. It's thought that Victorian artists invented this hat to help children to work out who the witch was in a picture.

The comb grew into a tangled forest and the witch could not fly through it.

23

Enter the WITCH-FINDERS

From the 1450s to the 1650s, witch-finding was big business in Europe. This was a time when belief in the supernatural reached its peak.

WITCH-SPOTTING HANDBOOK

In 1487, a book came out in Germany called *Malleus Maleficarum*, which means "The Hammer of Witches." It was translated into many languages and became a bestselling handbook that described how witches worked, how to recognize them, and how to punish them. It led to the rounding up of thousands of people who were sent for trial, accused of being witches.

The Hammer of Witches was a guidebook that witch-finders used for hundreds of years.

WITCH-FINDER GENERAL

The practice of witch-finding was strongest in Germany, but in the middle of the 1600s, it spread to England. A man called Matthew Hopkins started calling himself the Witch-finder General. He claimed to have a list of every witch in England.

No woman was safe as he hunted for witches. He tortured them and ducked them into water to see if they would float or sink. However, his good fortune came to a sudden stop in 1646 when he was criticized for his cruel methods and for charging too much.

HOPKINS. THE WITCH FINDER

Matthew Hopkins, the most notorious witch-finder in England.

Witch bottles

Superstitious people did strange things to protect themselves and their homes from witches. For example, they filled pottery bottles with human urine, hair, nail clippings, and pieces of iron. These so-called witch bottles were buried in the ground, where they had the power to break spells.

The Witch in the STONE BOAT

A long time ago, King Sigurd sailed the sea with his queen and their baby son. As Sigurd rested below deck, a strange boat pulled up alongside the ship.

The boat was made of stone, and was rowed by an ugly witch. She stripped the queen of her clothes and put them on. As she did, her wrinkles fell away, her bent nose became straight and she took on human form. She put the queen into the stone boat, and cast a spell to make it vanish into the cold, dark underworld.

The witch climbed on board and, unknown to King Sigurd, took the queen's place.

This story comes from
ICELAND

After a while, King Sigurd noticed that the queen had become stubborn and short-tempered and then, one day, he was visited by a woman in white who rose up through the floor, with a chain tied around her waist. The white woman cradled the baby tenderly and the king knew it was his true wife. He cut her binding chain with his sword. Free of the spell, she told Sigurd about the witch in the stone boat.

Sigurd released the queen from the spell, and went after the wicked witch.

Sigurd gathered the witch up into a sack. Stones were thrown at her until she was dead, and her body was torn to pieces and scattered to the four corners of the kingdom. She could never harm anyone ever again.

Witch weather

It was said that witches controlled the weather. They caused storms at sea by dumping the contents of their cauldrons into the water, and sank ships by hurling bolts of lightning at them. They trapped the wind in knots tied in ropes, then caused storms by untying the knots to release the energy.

27

Punishment for WITCHES

People who were accused of being witches were tortured, in order to force them to admit they were witches.

TORTURE

The accused were flogged or stretched on the rack until they felt their arms and legs would be pulled off. Their thumbs were placed into thumbscrews, and as the screws were tightened, pain shot through the bone.

In some cases, a **witch's cradle** was used. The person was bundled into a sack, which was tied to the branch of a tree. It was then made to swing and spin. The person felt dizzy and sick. Any form of torture only stopped when they confessed to being a witch.

Witches were subjected to terrible forms of torture.

NO SLEEP

Matthew Hopkins, England's Witch-finder General, kept his victims awake for days. If they began to fall asleep, their guards woke them up. When the victims could stand it no more, they admitted to being witches.

A woman accused of being a witch is asked to sign a confession, admitting her guilt.

In Europe in the Middle Ages, the fear of witches was so great that thousands of people were sentenced to death.

TRIAL AND SENTENCE

Having forced their victims to confess, a trial would be held. They were usually sentenced to death, executed by burning at the stake. In some cases, they were burned alive; in others they were strangled and then their bodies were burned until all that was left was ash.

Horseshoes

In the past, horseshoes were nailed to houses with their points turned downward, so that witches and other forms of evil would always fall out and never be allowed to enter the building.

TIMELINE

1275 A woman in France, Hugues de Baniol, became the first person known to have been burned as a witch.

1280 The first images appeared of a witch riding a broomstick.

1300–1330 Witch trials began in Europe.

1435–1450 The first major witch hunts began in many western European countries.

1487 A fact book called *Malleus Maleficarum* (The Hammer of Witches) was published and described how to hunt and destroy witches.

1550–1650 The "burning times," when trials and executions of witches reached a peak, mainly in France, Germany, and Switzerland.

1583 More than a hundred people were burned as witches over three months in Osnabruck, Germany.

1645 In England, Elizabeth Clarke became the first person accused by Witch-finder General Matthew Hopkins of being a witch.

1684 Alice Molland was the last person executed in England as a witch.

1692 Twenty people were executed as witches in Salem, Massachusetts.

1745 Father Louis Debaraz was the last person executed in France as a witch.

1775 Anna Maria Schwiigel became the last person executed in Germany as a witch.

1792 Poland became the last country in Europe to execute a person as a witch.

1997 *Harry Potter and the Philosopher's Stone*, the first book in the series, was published.

The Harry Potter series consists of seven books and eight movies.

GLOSSARY

ATHAME
A knife, sharpened along both edges, used by a witch to direct her power.

BLASTING
When a witch places a harmful spell on farmer's fields to stop them from producing crops.

CAULDRON
An iron cooking pot used by a witch to prepare potions.

DUCKING
A form of torture in which a person accused of being a witch was pushed under water.

FAMILIAR
A witch's companion, such as a cat, who acted as her spy.

GRIMOIRE
A book of spells.

HAG
An ugly old witch.

HAGSTONE
A stone that was thought to prevent witches from entering a house.

HALLOWEEN
All Hallows Eve, the night of October 31, when witches are at their most active.

SAMHAIN
A festival held on October 31 to mark the start of winter.

WISE WOMAN
A witch who uses her power to help, not to harm.

WITCH MARK
A mark on the skin, such as a spot, thought to show the person is a witch.

WITCH'S CRADLE
A form of torture in which a person accused of being a witch was spun around to make them dizzy.

WITCH'S LADDER
A short rope with knots tied in it by a witch. Each knot represented a spell.

INDEX